The Sadistically Clever and Sometimes Funny Writings of
Jeffrey Brian Romeo

Jeffrey Brian Romeo

authorHOUSE

AuthorHouse™
1663 Liberty Drive
Bloomington, IN 47403
www.authorhouse.com
Phone: 833-262-8899

Published by AuthorHouse 11/19/2024

ISBN: 979-8-8230-3418-0 (sc)
ISBN: 979-8-8230-3419-7 (hc)
ISBN: 979-8-8230-3417-3 (e)

Library of Congress Control Number: 2024924449

Print information available on the last page.

This book is printed on acid-free paper.

Contents

A Moment In Time

It's time to stand up and look that wound in the eye
See it for what it is and rise up to the sky

Ride with the wind on the back of the dragon
Sail on the seas and rule like a captain

We're here for the moment but never too long
We must be brave, courageous and strong

Bring me a flower and sing me a song
Stay with me forever until the music is gone

We live for the moment, a moment in time
Hold on to the day like the sweet sunshine

There's no time like the present better than now
To fight for honor and speak loudly and proud

Do not forget to hold your place in the line
Stand up for others and be merry and wise

We're here for the moment but never too long
We must be brave, courageous and strong

Bring me a flower and sing me a song
Stay with me forever until the music is gone

We live for the moment, a moment in time
Hold on to the day like the sweet sunshine

A Shot Heard 'Round The World

Uncle Sam and Betsy Ross
Nathanial Greene and Henry Knox

They poured the tea into the sea
For independence and liberty

Firecracker- firecracker
Boom- boom- boom
God and guns
Red, white and blue

A shot heard 'round the world gave us what we needed
The mighty tyrant lost and defeated

Paul Revere and George Washington
Ben Franklin and Peter Salem

They set the tone for all to know
That America was free from foe

Glory- glory
Hallelujah
Williamsport
Ticonderoga

A shot heard 'round the world gave us what we needed
The price we paid for stripes and freedom

About To Die

Like the sands of an hourglass
You can't outrun time
There's a price to pay yet
For the sins of your crime

It's a matter of life
And a matter of death
When the dark knight comes
Swallow your last breath

Before you eat the last meal
And you say your goodbye
Better say your blessing
Cuz you're about to die

When the fun time is over
It's time to take out the trash
You can sleep in the dark
With the bugs and the rats

At the end of the night
Only one thing's for sure

There is no overtime
Death is the final score

Before you hear the church bells
And you look to the sky
Better pray forgiveness
Cuz you're about to die

Aim For The Jugular

I'm a hunter and trapper in the cobweb of death
I creep up and bite you and suck out your breath

My mouth is like fire
It spits out a flame
Inject you with venom
Then I eat your brain

Aim for the jugular
Or right for the heart
I'm gonna mow you down
And tear you apart

I'm a killer and soldier in the movies you've seen
I march thru the jungle like a killing machine

My desk job is boring
So, I make up a story
About the havoc I caused
And my days of glory

Aim for the jugular
Or straight to the heart
I'm cocked hard and loaded
And razor sharp

Always Be Free

I'm alone again
I can't find my friends

The river flows
Under my toes
And I will always be free

I'm on the road
I'm headed home
And I will take you with me

My spirit talks
My spirit breathes
It's in my soul to believe

I'm immune to you
After all I've been thru

The moment grows
Just like a rose
And I will always be free

I'm a flying crow
I'm a flake of snow
And I will take you with me

My wings can fly
My wings can lift
It's my style to stay adrift

I don't mind
I'm doing fine
And I will always be free

A strong wind blows
My steel heart glows
And I will take you with me

Back In The Day

Well, I was a cool mother fucker in junior high
It was one of the best times of my life
I had friends to spare and girls to share
And they all had that stuck up hair

Well, I was one of the guys from the popular crew
We wore no socks with our shoes
There were gym classes and hall passes
And there were plenty of jack asses

Back in the day
When we had it all
It was MTV
And the Meadowbrook Mall

Back in the day
When we were kids
We picked up the phone
And called our friends

Well, I remember the parties and school dances
Spin the bottle and romances
Making dates on roller skates
Catechism classes at the old All Saints

Well, we always won the football games
Redskins, Warriors and the Braves
Nothing better than the 5th quarter
And interviews with TV reporters

Back in the day
When we had it all
It was MTV
And the Meadowbrook Mall

Back in the day
When we were kids
We picked up the phone
And called our friends

Battle Cries

To the east, we make our peace
To the west, we stop to rest

Is there any place in between
Somewhere to fill up my canteen

Shout for your mother
And call my name brother

I'll be there to take you home
We will never leave you alone

On the 4th we fly you high
For all the ones that gave their lives
Lightning bugs light up the sky
The rockets scream like battle cries

Rebels yelled as the bodies fell
Warriors danced as the front advanced

When duty called you were the first in line
Trading places with the ones that die

You deserve a Purple Heart
Recognition and a Silver Star

On the 4th we fly you high
For all the ones that gave their lives
Lightning bugs light up the sky
The rockets scream like battle cries

Better Off Dead

I can see the good times start to fade away
The high cloud you rode in on slowly turns to gray

Times are rough
Times are bad
Time for me
To make you sad

I need you like I need a hole in the head
An angry mob or a defiant kid
Loving you, I'm better off dead
Black-and-blue, or sick in bed

You moved in way too fast to make the kill
Now you're no longer suited to fit the bill

Times are poor
Times are crude
Time for me
To be bluntly rude

I need you like I need a hole in the head
An angry mob or a defiant kid
Loving you, I'm better off dead
Black-and-blue, or sick in bed

Black Heart

I am no saint
For I frolic in hate
I suffer from kuru
From the flesh that I ate

The wicked infects
And often injects
Tears out the inside
With tortured regrets

I am the blood, I am the pulse, I am the ghost in the dark
I prick and I pierce, and I rule with my black heart

I kill for no good and tear men apart
Choke with my hands, my fist and black heart

I am unholy
For I drink from the sea
I conceal from the light
So, you don't find me

The man I am not
Was paid for and bought
My rumors and gossip
Only thicken the plot

I am the past, I am the future, I am the end and the start
I stab and I thrust, and I rule with my black heart

I kill for no good and tear men apart
Choke with my hands, my fist and black heart

Black Scream

It's the nail hammered in the wall
It's a fight and a brawl
The never-ending punishment
That fucks inside us all

It's the wave that crashes in
It's a tattoo on the skin
The fist of Iron Mike
That punches you in the chin

Crashing cymbals
Roaring rumbles
Heavy metal growl machine

Rolling thunder
Charging power
Sounding like a black scream

It's the curse of the witch
It's a noise that makes you twitch
The soul of a man
That cries in perfect pitch

It's the howl of a hound
It's a dog that flees the pound
The eye of a storm
That blows me all around

Crashing cymbals
Roaring rumbles
Heavy metal growl machine

Rolling thunder
Charging power
Sounding like a black scream

Bonnie And Clyde

I met my match at age fifteen
She was a lean mean killing machine

Her frame of mind was a model B
She kept that motor running clean

Hellion, rebellions, fury
and skeletons
Always looking for a ride

Felons, possessions, fiery and evil ones
Like Bonnie and Clyde

I'm always ready for a getaway
Stash my bags and hideaway

We were the nation's public enemy
Filling our pockets with robberies

Hellion, rebellions, fury
and skeletons
Always looking for a ride

Felons, possessions, fiery and evil ones
Like Bonnie and Clyde

Always looking for a ride
Just like Bonnie and Clyde
When there's nowhere left to hide
I'd just rather die

Brilliant Fucking Plan

I took my beautiful date
To a holiday dance
But she forgot to tell me
One key thing in advance

The dude she dated 3 years
Up until last month
Well, he surely didn't like
Seeing me there that much

So, I tried to walk away
The gentleman that I am
But he got in my face
It was more than I could stand

I'll bury him deep if I can
Like a body in quicksand
Chop him into pieces
Such a brilliant fucking plan

I walked into the bank
Dressed up for Halloween
It wasn't my idea
To devise such a scheme

Yes, I've dined and dashed
And I stole some gasoline
But that was before camera phones
And I was only just a teen

I used to launder money
For the Italian mob
But I never killed anyone
That I've ever loved

I'll bury my crimes if I can
Like a body in quicksand
It made good sense at the time
Such a brilliant fucking plan

Oh, there is just one more thing
I may have failed to say
If the FBI is listening
Then this song was just for play

Camoflauged Deceit

Dress me up in a brand-new suit
A Cartier and wingtip shoes
I'll bring the words, you bring the news
I'll stare all night at the lovely views

Oh, the sun and moon, they make love in the afternoon
They charm the sky, they keep in tune
Like a fresh cool breeze in the month of June

I spread the gospel on god's green earth
Speak the language and go to church
I help the elderly cross the street
But I'm full of smiles and camouflaged deceit

I'm a friendly wolf that plays too rough
My dog like mind can't get enough
I take a bite, you share my stuff
Pet my back and feel my scruff

Oh, the web I weave, the wickedness of hungry thieves
I lead the way, they follow me
On a trail of bread and planted seeds

I spread the gospel on god's green earth
Speak the language and go to church
I help the elderly cross the street
But I'm full of smiles and camouflaged deceit

Cheapskate

Shotgun Mary is a big-time boozer
One time winner and a two-time loser

I can't help to stare
She don't seem to care

When she hits the stage
She don't act her age

I'm nothing but a tight cheapskate

Nicki darling is the star of the show
She turns the heat on high and the water flows

No need to check the clock
The night won't stop

When she takes the bait
She ain't no saint

I'm nothing but a cheap cheapskate

Child's Play

In the color of night in the city of lights
Everything is aglow and shining bright

Silent and still as the snow begins to fill
The streets with whiteness as the temperature chills

You can take me home again and make me whole
It reminds me of heaven
and the smell of burning coal

It's the simple things that hold me together
Like child's play and the Winter weather

My heart's desire warmed by the fire
Outside I can hear the sound of the choir

The stores are closed along with the roads
Family and pets stay in the comfort of home

You can take me home again and make me whole
It reminds me of heaven
and the smell of burning coal

It's the simple things that hold me together
Like child's play and the Winter weather

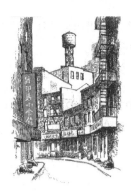

Chinatown Special

I got a hundred bucks and an itch to scratch
Brand new shoes and a purse to match

Living like a pimp under the streetcar lights
I got a mean bark, but I'm cool as ice

Ask me something and I'll give you nothing
I push and shove, but they keep on coming

Rolex watches and high price apparel
A fine example for the Chinatown special

I'm like a raging bull in a China shop
Breaking the rules until I never stop

Living like a worm in a bottle of boos
I catch more suckers than a ship of fools

Ask me something and I'll give you nothing
I fib and bluff, but they keep on coming

Gucci, Coach and Gabrielle
A fine example for the Chinatown special

Chinese Whispers

I speak the truth, but they repeat the lies
I've heard the message a million times

It's starts with peace and ends in war
This road to hell I've seen before

A war of words and enemy tricks
The next one will be fought with sticks

Secret codes and Chinese whispers
Dangerous minds and classroom thinkers

I come in peace but spread dissent
Like icing on a hot danish

SOS on the western front
The final fight slowly erupts

False accusations and more deep fakes
Bombers, jets and army tanks

Secret codes and Chinese whispers
Dangerous minds and classroom thinkers

Church On Sunday

Brother, sister, elder
Come hell or high water

Teach your children well
About church, heaven and hell

I got 40 wives but don't be jealous
They wear long skirts and silk blue bonnets

Living like a Saint
Every other day
I seek wisdom, morality
And church on Sunday

I'm on a rocky mountain high
It's like Christmas in July

The members of the compound
Own the temples and the town

I'm at the crossroads of the west
Where even the devil is quite impressed

Living like a Saint
Every other day
I seek good faith, humility
And church on Sunday

Convict Poker

I see you sitting there, just chomping at the bit
You may not like the odds, but the bull decides who wins

Sweat running down my brow, horns pointed at my back
I place my hands on the table and brace my body for impact

Stick to your convictions
Ace, King or Joker
I never thought I'd die
Playing convict poker

Place an apple on my head and take your best shot
Nothing makes me more nervous than a crooked cop

You read me like a book, my face is your next tell
I can play cards for hours, passing time in jail

Stick to your convictions
Ace, King or Joker
I never thought I'd die
Playing convict poker

I'm not just a funny clown, there's a reason for my candor
I like to take big risk, like a death-defying gambler

I'm not a jailbird chicken, a fish or a snitch
I'd rather bleed and die
Than be your little bitch

Stick to your convictions
Ace, King or Joker
I'm trying to survive
Playing convict poker

Convicted Felon

I'm a loner and stoner and I'm on the wrong track
Made one wrong turn now I can't find my way back

I'm a drinker and smoker and I'm addicted to crack
My bad habits are deadly like a STEM heart attack

I got caught buyin and sellin
Now I'm a convicted felon
I did some wheelin and dealin
Now I'm living in prison

I'm a beggar and stealer and I'm a thief in the night
When you go on vacation, I take whatever I like

I'm twisted and demented and I'm strapped to the heel
Make one false move and I shoot to kill

I got caught buyin and sellin
Now I'm a convicted felon
I did some wheelin and dealin
Now I'm living in prison

Crosswinds

Looking out my window
At the stars behind me
Reminders of the past
Every time I leave

New River Bridge
On south 19
I think of her
Every time I dream

Driving thru the clouds
Overtop the mountains
Higher than a child's kite
Flying in the crosswinds

We all know the feeling
Riding on inspiration
So, we keep on chasing
After our ambitions

Back and forth
Across the state line
We zig and zag
Straight thru life

Driving thru the clouds
Overtop the mountains
Higher than a child's kite
Flying in the crosswinds

Bridge-
Search deep into your soul
To see the light in the tunnel
For the challenge of life
Is worth every struggle

Daddy Always Told Me

I'm just a good ol boy- singing country roads
I got a job fixing tractors- and pickup trucks to load

There's nothing that can stop me- when it's quitting time
I take my daily paycheck- and buy myself a prime

My daddy always told me- no matter what you do
Put your money where your mouth is- or you'll end up getting
screwed

Working hard for the family- my shifts an all-day grind
I can't afford to take time off- or my bills get behind

I learned from watching my daddy- how to change a tire
He said hand me that lug wrench- and those fucking pliers

My daddy always told me- no matter what you do
Be careful with the ladies- they'll break your heart in two

I drink beer from the can- and Jim Beam from the bottle
Swallowed down my whiskey whore- like water from the nozzle

My daddy always told me- no matter what you do
Be careful with the ladies- or you'll end up getting screwed

Dead, Gone and Dearly Departed

Running from the man
Catch me if you can
Ain't the first time
I've been on the stand

I swear to tell the truth
There's nothing I won't do
With my hand on the Bible
I've been falsely accused

Dead, gone and dearly departed
Life without parole, don't get much harder

Dead, gone, and dearly departed
Listen God, I need a pardon

One night in that prison
I learned a new religion
In order to survive
I had to become a villain

I filled out the disclaimer
Got nailed by the hammer
I'm just a little tied up
Spending time in the slammer

Dead, gone, and dearly departed
If I have to die, I don't want to be a martyr

Dead, gone, and dearly departed
Listen God, I need a pardon

Deadly Eyes

Always there to lift me up
Happy as a buttercup

Frisky as a cat and mouse
Playing chase through the house

Perfect as the earth's sunrise
Killer looks and deadly eyes

I was looking for a ray of shine
When she caught me with those deadly eyes

Tailor made like a unique bouquet
Smelling fresh on a summer day

A treasure chest of hope and faith
Protected like a hotel safe

Perfect as the earth's sunrise
Killer looks and deadly eyes

I was looking for a ray of shine
When she caught me with those deadly eyes

Demons On Parade

They look like you and me
Face, head and spine
But they put on their pants
Two legs at a time

The world's oldest profession
Was born with a lie
Promises- promises
Until the day that we die

It looks likes death out my window
I hear a hundred thousand feet
The demons on parade
March to a different beat

They whistle when they work
Lips, tongue and air
But they sing a different tune
So, think twice and beware

The gods of the parliament
Been pulling the strings
Freezing in hell
Since death was a thing

Doctor Grim knocks on my door
I'm afraid to fall asleep
The demons on parade
Stomping thru the street

Devil in the Details

After all that we've been thru
Dating, life and risky business
I'm glad we can still be friends
And still have some benefits

When you're feeling lonely
Forgotten, empty and blue
You can call me up at night
For a needed hug or two

The devil is in the details
Be sure to read the fine print
It could just be another trap
So, enter at your own risk

After all the things we said
The promises and high hopes
I'm glad we can still be associates
And end it on a good note

You still got my number
It's written in your phone
I know you think about it
When you're all alone

The devil is in the details
Be sure to read the fine print
It could just be another trap
So, enter at your own risk

Devil's Lounge

Down the staircase
Around the bend
Round and round
It never ends

Fall from grace
Into the ditch
Dig in deeper
Like a trench

Look into the eyes of a snake pit and you will see a nightmare
going down
The venom sinks deeper with every heartbeat as you play with
fire in the devil's lounge

Trust no one here
Thru the maze
Another trick
To fool the way

Rise and shine
Forget the past
Hear the echoes
Of an evil laugh

Look into the eyes of a snake pit and you will see a nightmare
going down
The venom sinks deeper -with every heartbeat as you play with
fire in the devil's lounge

Smoke and fire
Rain and blood
Ice and hail
Wind and floods

Disinclined

I got a case of beer and my cigarettes
Down all 9 lives but I ain't dead yet

Took a shot of venom at the whiskey bar
Started some trouble but it went too far

If I'm wrong, I'm wrong but I know I'm right
I get anxious, nervous and all uptight

Out of line- out of mind
No control- I'm disinclined

I can't believe what they're doing to me
The more I fight the more I bleed

I lost my head and never looked back
I'm out of date and all off track

If I'm wrong, I'm wrong but I know I'm right
I get anxious, nervous and all uptight

Out of line- out of mind
No control- I'm disinclined

I took dead aim, but I missed the mark
I'm the new top dog in the trailer park

Out of line- out of mind
No control- I'm disinclined

Dog Days

I want to be her top dog and sleep in her bed
I don't have fleas and I don't fucking shed

I may sleep in late and snore like pig
But I don't give a crap or shit where I live

I'd be faithful and loyal right by her side
Obedient and tame until the day I die

Swimming in the puddles of raindrops and love
The dog days of summer have just begun

I'm a husky fella, loving and smart
Playful and scruffy with a lion's heart

I may be cute but I'm bad to the bone
Man's best friend in her safety zone

Life with her would be a walk in the park
Special treats whenever I bark

Swimming in the puddles of raindrops and love
The dog days of summer have just begun

Down On The Farm

I got an old axe to grind
And some egos to chop
I live deep in the woods
With the grain and the crops

I get all dressed up to kill
Got my camo and boots
You never see me coming
I aim and then I shoot

Up in the hills and down on the farm
I got high tech surveillance with traps and alarms

Up in the hills and down on the farm
I got a 12-gauge shotgun under my arm

I got twenty-seven cousins
Nine uncles and five aunts
On a farm in Kentucky
With a dog named Old Champ

We bootleg and we smuggle
Make a promise to deliver
Fire up white lightening
The fruits of our labor

Up in the hills and down on the farm
I got high tech cameras with traps and alarms

Up in the hills and down on the farm
I got Smith and Wesson under my arm

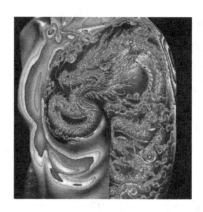

Dragon Fire Tattoo

The pain of a thousand stitches sewing my leg together
Sketches on my skin will grow and last forever

Black work- Grey work
Detailed- Artwork

Half sleeve- Full sleeve
Pull up- My sleeve

Guess what- Guess who
Shipwrecked- Tattoo

Guess what- Guess who
Dragon fire- Tattoo

The lines are sharp and straight and pointy as an arrow
Filling in the spaces with shades of smoke and shadows

Old school- New school
Hooky- No school

Stab me- Jab me
I love- Agony

Guess what- Guess who
Shipwrecked- Tattoo

Guess what- Guess who
Dragon fire- Tattoo

Dragon Hands

Heated moments breathing down my back
Unleashing fury like a shark attack

Flying over the hunting grounds
Consumption up by leaps and bounds

Bigger than life and flying free
Imagination and effigies

Melt my heart, tear me apart
You stole my valor, right from the start

Powerful jaws and long sharp claws
Dragon hands that cut like saws

Dubbed the prince of fear and darkness
Known for tricks and being obnoxious

Breathing fire and enormous power
Devouring sheep every other hour

Captivating a large audience
Burning ships and tearing flesh

Melt my heart, tear me apart
You stole my valor, right from the start

Powerful jaws and long sharp claws
Dragon hands that cut like saws

Eighteen

Long hair, tattoos and the sound of heavy metal

My fist held high shouting to hell with the devil

I still love my hair bands but I ain't no sentimental

I'm a crowd surfing hellion riding shotgun in the barrel

Yea I was eighteen once
That's when I learned to drink, smoke, and cuss

Yea I was eighteen once
Growing up fast ain't worth all the fuss

I used to be a handful and stay up late all night

Now I'm an early riser and go to church to feel alright

Yea I was eighteen once
That's when I learned to fight, love, and cuss

Yea I was eighteen once
Making your own bed ain't worth all the fuss

Everything is Darkness

I'm searching for a resting place
Like a sword that seeks a scabbard
I find myself a haunted inn
Where the phantasms still gather

What are you like in a room
Alone and all by yourself
Are you scared and insecure
Do you eat from the inside out

Hair white as snow
Eyes dark as coal
Everything is darkness
My body weak and old

Everything is darkness
When the clock no longer chimes
Everything is darkness
When the light no longer shines

A story told from hand me downs
Of an old man and his castle
Anchored in the harbor
Like a ship without a battle

How is it that you can see so well
When there's nothing up ahead
Are you certain and optimistic
About the roadmaps that you read

Many stories told
Of blood turning cold
Everything is darkness
My nucleus exposed

Everything is darkness
When you hear the sobbing cries
Everything is darkness
When the fingers close your eyes

Family Man

If you want to fly you must realize
The sky is where our freedom lies

Walk with me towards liberty
Protect your nest like a bumble bee

I'm a family man
I do all that I can
I go to church
And I say yes ma'am

I'm a family man
I do all that I can
I watch Fox News
And I'm a Yankees fan

It's ok if you want to pray
For a better life and a better way

I love baseball and a good pub crawl
Classic rock and I obey the law

I'm a family man
I do all that I can
I go to church
And I say yes ma'am

I'm a family man
I do all that I can
I'm a father first
And I'm American

Fire In The Sky

I'll have another whiskey and cigarette
I got the time to spare

Choke on this and swallow it
I'm not the type to care

Jägermeister, whiskey or gin
Open up honey and let me in

Lord, you're killing me
Nothing can stop me now
Sit back and watch me baby
Let me show you how

White lightening, fire in the sky
Drinking with you baby always gets me high

I got the best seat in the house tonight
I'll be here until the end

Looking good and feeling right
Plenty of money to spend

Alabama slammer on the tip of my tongue
Liquid cocaine and 151

Lord, you're calling me
Nothing can stop me now
Sit back and watch me baby
Let me show you how

White lightening, fire in the sky
Drinking with you baby always gets me high

Bridge-
Start a fight or start a brawl, I hold my cup until last call
Crash my car or hit the wall, I fill my cup and drink it all

Frankenstein's Bride

I met this girl online and figured uh what could go wrong
She liked music and sports so I thought we would get along

Then the clock struck midnight and the alcohol wore off
She started making wedding plans and acting like the boss

Just when I thought it couldn't get any worse
I hit rock bottom and got swept up in the current

Just when I thought it couldn't get any worse
I met Frankenstein's bride, now I suffer the curse

Five kids later, two dogs and a recent divorce
My girlfriend's pregnant and I got buyer's remorse

I still got my van and my dogs down by the river
Living like a rat on a ship but I'm 5 times better

Just when I thought it couldn't get any worse
I hit rock bottom and got swept up in the current

Just when I thought it couldn't get any worse
I met Frankenstein's bride, now I suffer the curse

Game Of Thrones

Dance with the dragons in the house of flames
Ruling seven Kingdoms is the greatest game

Crows, cowards, rooks and pawns
Are the weakest link when the swords are drawn

Rock and stone
Ash and bone
You think you know grief
Welcome to the game of thrones

Facing family drama, life and death
Kissed by fire and dragons' breath

Blood, guts, sweat and tears
Burning cities for a thousand years

Rock and stone
Ash and bone
You think you know grief
Welcome to the game of thrones

God Willing

I got too much love to give
And not enough time to live
But I'm still trying

Wake me up to survive
And keep my plans alive
Yea I'm still striving

Someday it will come
Someday you will see
It will all be fine
God willing let it be

I got a mind to articulate
And a heart that will detonate
Like a torpedo

My feelings strike a chord
And I try not to ignore
Everything I know

Someday it will come
Someday you will see
It will all be fine
God willing let it be

Bridge-
The sun will warm you up and the rain will make you wet
True love will grow your heart like Romeo and Juliette

Good Girls Do

It ain't always easy to let your guard down
But when it comes to loving, I'm the best in town

One, two, three
Won't ya listen to me
Four, five, six
Try to pick up chicks

From Jersey shore
To Kalamazoo
Everywhere I go honey
Good girls do

If you like what you hear and you like what you see
Then let down your hair and come home with me

Seven, eight, nine
Champagne and wine
Ten, eleven, twelve
Toast to good health

From the Big Easy
To Timbuktu
Everywhere I look baby
Good girls do

Work all day and stay up all night
Drink High Noon, play nice and fight

They start off slow, but they finish strong
Now it's time for you to just go along

One, two, three
Baby if you please
Four, five, six
Turn on the Netflix

From Taylor Swift
To me and you
Everyone does it baby
Good girls too

Groundhog Day

I've seen it all before
The signs I can't ignore

Stop, do not enter, rough road ahead
Dips, bumps and slippery when wet

Up and down the highway of life
Can't make up my mind or decide

Where I'm going or where I been
Groundhog Day is here again

Lost in my own shadow
Stuck in a deep burrow

Rain, sunshine and cloudy skies
From the lowest lows to the highest highs

Winter days and early Spring
Warm enough for the birds to sing

It's that time of year my friend
Groundhog Day is here again

Hand To Hold

They build you up and then they cut you down
They act on your side but then they sleep around

I don't need no complications
Unkind words or agitation
I just need a hand to hold
Love, hope and satisfaction

I don't need no more cut throats
Snap chat, Instagram or FB post
I just need a hand to hold

They come to me, and I hold my breath
They squeeze tight and crush me half to death

I don't need no box of rocks
Headaches or stumbling blocks
I just need a hand to hold
24-7 and around the clock

I don't need no more sugar coats
Red flags, lies or Dear John notes
I just need a hand to hold

Happy As A Child

I play golf all day and take power naps so I can stay up late at night

I take my sweet time and I spend it wise so I can live out my best life

Life is short so make it count
Remember what it's like to be a kid

Kiss the girls and roll the dice
Stay free and cool like the wind

Dogs in skirts and funny shirts
Make me giggle, laugh and smile
Hula hoops and mini coupes
Make me happy as a child

I roam the streets like an alley cat so I can do what I do best

I sneak around and I get off easy just like the teacher's pet

Life is short so make it grand
Remember your friends you met in school

They knew you well and had your back
When you used to break the rules

Dogs in skirts and funny shirts
Make me giggle, laugh and smile
Hula hoops and mini coupes
Make me happy as a child

Heart Attacks and
Sneak Attacks

One day in Jonestown
I was there to mess around
Listening to the weirdos
Preach, drink and drown

Headed to the clinic
It will only take a minute
To get a new prescription
And clear my bumpy skin

Heart attacks and sneak attacks
Jim Jones, fools and crazy Jacks

Commies, Marxist and Socialist
They think they know better
All they really want
Is all your money, goods and power

We don't need a part time doctor
Or a make-believe preacher

I'm running for President
Like a natural born leader

The world is full of lunatics
They think the rule the land
All they really want
Is for you to jump at their command

Heart attacks and sneak attacks
Jim Jones, fools and crazy Jacks

Heaven And Nature

I can smell the leaves when the trees shed their skin
See an image of God in the clouds above the mountains

I can hear the creeks running through the rolling hills
Feel the power of the water turning those old creek mills

Wake me up it's time to shine
Rivers of gold and evergreen pines
Mountain tops and deep coal mines
A place heaven and nature can intertwine

I woke up to the sound of insects and wood being chopped
A breeze strong enough to blow me off the mountain top

My friends and I are coming home to converge and reunite
We are going to celebrate our heritage for at least one more
night

Wake me up it's time to shine
Rivers of gold and evergreen pines
Mountain tops and deep coal mines
A place heaven and nature can intertwine

Hell's Coming With Me

Like a storm in a teacup
I was born to raise hell
Drinking from the bottle
And the bottom of the well

I'm armed, lit and dangerous
Ruthless, guile and mean
You may see me on the news
Or running from the scene

I'm quick, deadly and menacing
Heartless, cruel and obscene
You tell them that I'm coming
And hell's coming with me

I never met anyone else
That drank as much as me
Until I met Jack Daniels
And his crew from Tennessee

I'm cold, hungry and desperate
Heinous, harsh and wicked

Make no mistake about it
I'm tormented and afflicted

I'm quick, deadly and menacing
Heartless, cruel and obscene
You tell them that I'm coming
And hell's coming with me

Hot To Trot

I'm not sure what took me so long
To say hello or to go for broke

Maybe it was the intimidation or just my crazy imagination but
whatever it was, I now feel a good sensation

When you're hot you're hot and when you're not you're not
I like it baby when you take charge on top

I come to you, and you pick the spot
When you dance for me, you're hot to trot

I saw you here and I saw you there
I knew one day I'd find a way

Maybe I feared the confrontation or some type of complication
but whatever it was, now I feel a fascination

When you're hot you're hot and when you're not you're not
That's right baby show me what you got

You smile at me, and I take my shot
You got to know, you're hot to trot

I Don't Wear A Leash

Life on the edge
Love on the run
Can't make this up
I'm just having fun

No more coke
No more dope
All my days
Went up in smoke

Out of sight out of mind
Out of bounds out of line

I'm still hard to reach
Hear me speak
I may be a dog
But I don't wear a leash

I share my love
She spreads her wings
When it all goes down
I just keep on coming

Love me
Or hate me
I'll take you
To destiny

Break up to make up
Shut up and pay up

I'm still hard to reach
Hear me speak
I may be a dog
But I don't wear a leash

I'm a male in heat
Trick for a treat
I rule the streets
And I don't wear a leash

I Must Be Scottish

Night after night I get wasted
Cock-eyed intoxicated

Brandy, wine and Tequila
A case of beer and amnesia

Started drinking in the middle of day
Oh lord I'm gonna have hell to pay

By 5 o'clock I'm demolished
I sit at the bar and get polished

By 9 o'clock I'm abolished
Dear god I must be Scottish

Day after day I get blasted
Smashed-drunk inebriated

Whiskey, beer and cider
About 35 milliliters

I just don't know when to say when
Oh lord I'm gonna miss work again

By 5 o'clock I'm demolished
I sit at the bar and get polished

By 9 o'clock I'm abolished
Dear god I must be Scottish

I Want That Girl

I saw her today at the gym- on the Nordic treadmill incline
She was pretty, athletic and slim- running all thru my mind

She caught me looking twice- so I stared off into space
I pretended to exercise- as I rode my bike in place

I want that girl to be my girl, but she thinks I am a creep
I want that girl to be my girl, but she thinks I'm old and weak

I saw her today at the Target- walking up and down the aisles
She was looking for a bargain- and I was trying to catch a smile

I followed her to sports and fitness- where I got surrounded
by security
She thought I looked suspicious- so the retired cop
embarrassed me

I want that girl to be my girl, but she thinks I am a creep
I want that girl to be my girl, but she thinks I'm old and weak

Bridge-
I saw you today, but I had nothing to say
I should have said hi before I got dragged away

Ice Cream Sunday

We go to church
And watch football
Play some golf
And make family phone calls

We go to the beach
And swim in the bay
Enjoy a cold treat
Like an ice cream Sunday

We clean the house
And make our beds
A fun game night
And dinner with friends

We meet up at brunch
For bacon and eggs
Enjoy life's heartbeat
Like an ice cream Sunday

We cut the grass
And trim the weeds
Change the oil
And pile up the leaves

We walk in the park
Sing, dance and play
Eat sweet candy
Like and ice cream Sunday

We jump from a boat
And fish off the hook
Go to bed early
And read a good book

The day of all days
Is Sunday funday
A day to relax
Like an ice cream Sunday

I'd Rather Be Dead

We had some good times
And we had some fun
She may look like Pamela
But she wasn't the one

She had a great job
And owned her own house
Watched football and golf
But I still had my doubts

She looked great in blue jeans
And fine in a dress
Dam pretty in pink
But she smoked cigarettes

I've searched long and hard
Yea that's what she said
But If I can't find the perfect woman then I'd rather be dead

She was wild in bed
And knew how to kiss
Complimented my ego
But she drank like a fish

She was half my age
And twice as grown up
Checked out other women
But she didn't vote Trump

She had the best shot
And knew all my weaknesses
Pretended to like my music
But was just too high maintenance

I've had beauty queens
Sleeping in my bed
But if I can't find the perfect woman for me I'd rather be dead

I'm not some kind of player
I'm just a cold heartbreaker
But honey if you call me baby too soon we'll that's a big deal
breaker

You know I have a few layers
I'm a mover and shaker
But honey if you want me to go to church well you don't have
a prayer

If Looks Could Kill

Buy me a double
Fill up my cup
Baby you know the drill
Just light me one up

Grab me a bottle
Pass it around
Baby you know the drill
We drink til we drown

I'll take me another
I'm not suicidal
But baby if looks could kill
I'd be dead on arrival

I'll take me another
I'm not homicidal
But baby if looks could kill
I'd be dead on arrival

Show me some courage
Never stand down
Baby you know the drill
Don't throw in the towel

Pour me a stiff one
Get me all hammered
Baby you know the drill
Play me some Haggard

I'll take me another
I'm not suicidal
But baby if looks could kill
I'd be dead on arrival

I'll take me another
I'm not homicidal
But baby if looks could kill
I'd be dead on arrival

If You Can't Beat em Kill em

No one likes to lose
But if you can't win by the rules
You take a rooftop position
Make earth shaking news

By any means necessary
Deep state or military
Infectious poison apples
Total revolutionary

Listen to me friend
I know you'd do anything to win
You said the quiet part out loud
If you can't beat em kill em

They're coming for your children
With tainted penicillin
Spying on your grandma
And American civilians

It's like the Wild Wild West
Law fare and arrest
The nation sinking fast
With wars and counter protest

Listen to me friend
I know you'd do anything to win
You said the quiet part out loud
If you can't beat em kill em

Nothing to lose cuz you already lost
Cheat, lie and steal like it's nobody's fault
You took dead aim, but you missed your mark
The conservative movement is under assault

If You Press

I'm a man of many faces
Simple but complicated

A jokester and a flirt
Like sunshine up your skirt

I promise you tomorrow
Give back yesterday
I got no time for sorrow
If you press, I walk away

I'm your future with no plans
A wall clock with no hands

The thoughts inside your head
Make my face turn hot and red

I'm sorted as a shuffle
Prevalent and all the rage
The hustle and the bustle
If you press, I turn the page

I'm Not What You Deserve

There goes my blood pressure
With my bad behavior
I feel my pulse begin to drum

All my respiration
It's an indication
For when I'm about to come

I like a fancy girl
I like some hips and curves
When I'm done with you
I'm not what you deserve

You're here for joy and pleasure
Cocaine, whips and leather
Your body fits me like a glove

I'm back in circulation
I'm into strangulation
It's the way I make sweet love

I like a fancy girl
I like some hips and curves
When I'm done with you
I'm not what you deserve

I grab my pipe and wear my robe
You take a shower and find your clothes

Just Like Easter Sunday

Wake up beautiful world
It's time to rise and shine
Open up the windows
Let the sun and breeze combine

When you hear the birds sing
About the paths they have flown
You get that funny feeling
And you know you're not alone

Just like Easter Sunday
I'm off to church again
Drink my tea and coffee
Be forgiven for my sins

The sun always shines
Even when it rains
It points in the direction
Away from all the flames

When his children gather
It reminds us of the good
He tackles all the trouble
Come and see where he stood

Just like Easter Sunday
I sing along to the hymns
Visit a farmers' market
And gather with my friends

Life Gone Wild

Look me in the eyes
When you tell those lies

Like the time you said
I was a cheap crackhead

You got more stories than a fable book
More stolen goods than a crooked crook

You're on my mind and in my head
Sailing by me on a traveling ship

Wave goodbye if you see me child
I'll be navigating thru a life gone wild

Oh, those big green eyes
In the dead of night

They hide the truth
When I search for clues

You break me down like a broken box
Crack my skull with a bag of rocks

You're in my heart and in my sights
Flying high and taking flight

Wave goodbye if you see me child
I'll be hanging on this life gone wild

Like A Hank Williams Song

Well, she threw out all my stuff
So, I had to sleep out in my truck
I think she finally had enough

Even the dogs won't look at me
I can tell they are displeased
And blame me for all their fleas

I thought I did everything right
But oh lord I was wrong
I got the lovesick blues
Like a Hank Williams song

I thought I would never leave
But oh lord I'm traveling on
I got the honky-tonk blues
Like a Hank Williams song

Well now I'm all out of luck
Like I lost a million bucks
And I'm living in my trunk

Even my friends all blame me
We cross swords and disagree
They stay away like I'm TNT

I thought I did everything right
But oh lord I was wrong
I got the lovesick blues
Like a Hank Williams song

I thought I would never leave
But oh lord I'm traveling on
I got the honky-tonk blues
Like a Hank Williams song

Little Doll

Nothing good happens after midnight unless you're home safe with me
I've been up all-night thinking about my little wanna be

Hour by hour, minute by minute, the seconds tick away

Whenever I'm with you, there's not enough time in the day

You know all my passwords and my door is always open
Come inside little doll, bring that love and emotion

All your mystery and promises are just another tease
That keep me waiting up to hear the jingle of your keys

Hour by hour, minute by minute, the seconds tick away

Whenever I'm with you, there's not enough time in the day

You know all my secrets, ambitions and desires
Come inside little doll, bring your passion and your fire

Little Johnny

A whisper in the shadow, a poor child on the run
The trials and tribulations of growing up a bastard son

Could I be the son of a King
The rightful heir to a dynasty
Could he be my neighbor
Or a menace to society

Here comes little Johnny
The spawn of polyamory
A superficial love child
Lust and pure fantasy

Never knowing truth or fiction, always facing persecution
His mother learned to cope with a life of prostitution

Could I be the son of an artist
The offspring of someone rich
Could he be in a band
Or a royal fucking dick

Here comes little Johnny
The spawn of polyamory
A superficial love child
Lust and pure fantasy

Long Live The King

Cut the head off from the snake and the body will regrow
But his memories remain just the same as the old

You can suck the blood like the mouth of a leach
But the brain controls the jaws that continue to speak

Give me death or victory
Stalemate, war and history
Celebrate, dance and sing
Long live the King

You can sell me down the river and betray my loyal trust
But never turn your back on the leopards that you hunt

Swim with the big fish in the wake of the pond
Like the butterfly stroke, graceful as a swan

Give me death or victory
Stalemate, war and history
Celebrate, dance and sing
Long live the King

Love Gone Mad

You been nothing but trouble since you came into my life
I should have learned my lesson baby the second time

Now I'm not made for your drama and your telling lies
I don't need you showing up here like a big surprise

I loved you once, I loved you twice
Now I'm broke, I paid the price
I loved you good, I loved you bad
Loving you, is love gone mad

I've seen all your ups and downs and highs and lows
And experienced your many fits and episodes

I don't need no boiling rabbits in my pots and pans
Or movie quotes from silence of the lambs

I loved you once, I loved you twice
Now I'm broke, I paid the price
I loved you good, I loved you bad
Loving you, is love gone mad

Love Me Or Hate Me

Smooth, swift and clever, aways on the go
Like Wylie coyote and the road runner show

Complex contraptions and animal instincts
Chasing down my dreams but never catching shit

Faster than a greyhound, smarter than a fox
Hungry as a hippo, stronger than an ox

I'm a bug on the windshield
A snake on the plane
Love me or hate me
I'll be sure to entertain

I would do anything to capture your heart
Even strap me to a jet and blow myself apart

All of my hard work seems to go unnoticed
The way you ignore me turns me into road dust

Devious and cunning, I've reached a plateau
My legs growing weak, I'm probably too old

I'm a bug on the windshield
A snake on the plane
Love me or hate me
I'll be sure to entertain

Love Soirée

Sitting here all alone
Counting up my wealth
Glancing thru my records
Sipping bottles from the shelf

The song that you wrote for me
Makes me smile with my eyes
The message that you left me
Could make a strong man start to cry

It's a hotel love soirée
A romantic way to say
I want to lay you down
Like an intimate cliche

Hearing voices on my phone
Telling stories to the chair
Staring her up and down
Venting about my affairs

The time you spent with me
Made me sick to let you go
The stories that you told me
Could make me want to bring you home

It's a hotel love soirée
A romantic way to say
I want to lay you down
Like an intimate cliche

Man On The Corner

The man on the corner is poor and hungry
He came to this land for milk and honey

Worked his fingers to the bone for blood money
Now he lives on the street and it ain't too funny

Living it up
Night after night
Same old story
Fight after fight

I don't have a job, a car or healthcare
I can't buy a home, rent, or a place to share

I'm the man on the corner, the man on the street
I'm your next-door neighbor, you don't want to meet

The man on the corner is breaking bad
He lives in a world of hurt and oh so sad

The urban grind made him go apeshit mad
Now he lost his wage and he ain't too glad

My bank is empty
I'm running on fumes
My credit's lousy
I'm all out of fuel

I don't have a job, a car or healthcare
I can't buy a home, rent, or afford to share

I'm the man on the corner, the man on the street
I'm your next-door neighbor that cries to sleep

Master

I know you want to sink your teeth into me, chew me up and drag me into the sea

I know you want to hold me down under and watch my blood bleed into the water

I see your eyes glow in the dark of night, you can hear me breathing ever so slight

Master of disguise- Ready to fight
Spinning death- I can feel you bite

The beating wings and buzzing bees, here they come chasing after me

I know you want to rule the world's economy, just like you subdued an entire colony

I can sense your path of self-destruction; I've been caught up in all your sticky corruption

Master of drones- Ready to spring
Swarming death- I can feel you sting

Bridge-
I can feel your bite, I can feel you sting
I can feel the heartache that you bring
It hurts so good, it hurt so bad
It hurts like I've been shot and stabbed

Mirror Mirror

Mirror, mirror I must confess
She makes my heart a boiling mess

She spins around with great finesse
Like a beauty queen in a dazzling dress

Mirror, mirror I must admit
Her company is the greatest gift

So many strengths I could make a list
But it's her eyes and smile I can't resist

Mirror, mirror I must do tell
I've been captured in her wonder spell

She rides along on the oceans swell
Like a dolphin playing with conch seashells

Mirror, mirror I must reveal
The way she touches and makes me feel

She turned my dreams into something real
Woke me up with romantic appeal

Misfit

I can feel your eyes on the back of my head
Looking for a reason to level up my meds

Round peg, square hole
Nut jobs and wackos
I'm the kind of misfit that acts like a psycho

I never seem to fit in the crowd you love to stay
Watching from my window as the kids run and play

Offbeat, out of control
Crackpots and weirdos
I'm the kind of misfit that acts like a sicko

I've been banned and disowned on the outside looking in
Treated for depression and self-scratches on my skin

Deranged and hysterical
Neurotic and delusional
I'm the kind of misfit that acts like a criminal

More Than Meets The Eye

I may not be what you think but at least I had a thought
Is it any wonder how the animals evolved

I know there's something inside those tiny stars that keeps
them shining bright
Like each blade of grass I cut, there's more than meets the eye

There may be another world but nothing like we know
Traveling thru the universe a million years ago

I know there's something clicking inside my head that keeps
me thinking all night
Like each rock in the sand I see, there's more than meets
the eye

Movie Night

It's you and me and a cooler makes three
Blanket, pillow and destiny

She was just 18
And homecoming queen

Found a good place under the stars
Down by the lake wrapped in my arms

I'm feeling alright
It's like a movie night

It's 3am, mama said where you been
I was out with Jeff at the old drive-in

He was sweet and nice
And is just my type

In the back of my truck, we got a little crazy
It was the first time I said I love you baby

Do you feel alright
It's like a movie night

Staying out late with my foxy prom date
I was on top of the world in 1988

Never wanted it to end
She still my dearest friend

You can take me back to the good old days
Sunday's school and matinees

Hold me tight
On a movie night

Moving On

I'm gonna pour my heart and rinse out my soul
Save my evil ass and learn self-control

Bury all my hatchets and move on with business
Embrace all my powers and erase the sickness

Moving on is harder than you think
But if you don't swim then you sink
Life is good life is sweet
But you can miss it all if you blink

Settle up my debts and pay for transgressions
Acknowledge all the facts with my last confession

I'm gonna keep it real so you can understand
Lay may cards on the table and take back command

Moving on is harder than you think
But if you don't swim then you sink
Life is good life is sweet
But you can miss it all if you blink

Murder She Wrote

I'm the wrong number in the bathroom stall
The dark shadow crawling on the wall

I'm the smoke and mirror at the old dive bar
The blood and the scab on your deepest scar

Murder she wrote
Cut my throat
Hanging free
At the end of my rope

I'm the weeds in the grass when you cut the lawn
The master of deceit and the devil's spawn

I'm the spirit in the bottle when you drink alone
The hammer and fist that breaks the bones

Murder she wrote
Got no hope
Flying free
Like a friendly ghost

You call to me when you're feeling weak
Devour dreams from the souls you seek

You steal from grace when the guards come down
Dig the graves at the end of the town

My Little Pony

I don't need any special gifts as long as I have you
When you're right here by my side there's nothing I can't do

The way you laugh, the way you smile sets the sunlight free
With plenty of your dazzle shining bright all over me

Wild horses and brown eyed ponies incredibly strong and proud
Playing in the open fields galloping all around

I'll lead the way, you follow me
Darling child, you'll always be
Running hard, racing free
My little girl, my little pony

You're a wildflower full of life branching out like a tree
I know you want to see the world and sail the deep blue sea

The way you grow, the way you stretch reaching for the stars
Soon you'll be a grown-up kid driving your own car

Wild horses and brown eyed ponies incredibly strong and proud
Playing in the open fields galloping all around

I'll lead the way, you follow me
Darling child, you'll always be
Running hard, racing free
My little girl, my little pony

No Feelings

Stuck in the mess
Down in a hole
Cut off from the world
Alone in the cold

Just give this old man a break
I made an innocent mistake
I'm feeling no feelings
But misery and heartache

Afraid of the dark
Caught in a trap
Lost in the wilderness
Thrown out with the scraps

Just need someone to blame
I can't remember her name
I'm feeling no feelings
But remorseful and shame

No Way To Die

Left there all alone
On the side of the road
Flesh and limbs torn apart

No one hears you groan
Or picks up broken bones
Crows and hawks eat your heart

That's no way to live and no way to die
Being eaten in the desert like a piece of pie

No way to live and no way to die
It shall be done like an eye for an eye

In the heat of the day
Or under the cover of shade
The carcass rots away

Stuck in lost and found
Tiny pieces on the ground
All the vultures invade

That's no way to live and no way to die
Being eaten in the desert like a piece of pie

No way to live and no way to die
It shall be done like an eye for an eye

Oceans Of Time

The magic on your face is all that I seek
When we play all day and walk on the beach

Adriatic and Mediterranean
Black, Red and Caspian
The original seven seas including the Persian and the Indian

The oceans of time
And the oceans of the world
I'd sail from coast to coast
To bring the gifts you deserve

The wag in your tail as we razzle and dazzle
Windows down on the highways we travel

North, South and Atlantic
East, West and the Pacific
The conventional seven seas including the subzero Arctic

The oceans of time
And the oceans of the world
I'd sail from coast to coast
To bring the gifts you deserve

Oh Sweet Sunshine

I got a secret little crush, in the apple of my eye
A mermaid, unicorn and a rainbow flying high

I got more things to say, about how sweet she really is
Like a genie in a bottle, she granted all my wishes

Living in a house, touched by her sweet hands
Concrete, bricks and sunshine
A future with big plans

Oh, sweet sunshine- Don't cry
And please don't go away
Oh, sweet sunshine- Be mine
And brighten up my day

She's got me singing in the shower, chirping like a bird
Running down the aisles, skipping like a girl

She's got a tender loving soul, and a heart that can't be beat
Dancing in the moonlight, shagging in the streets

Living in a dream, where everything comes true
Happiness and sunshine
And Superman protects you

Oh, sweet sunshine- Don't cry
And please don't go away
Oh, sweet sunshine- Be mine
And brighten up my day

One Hell Of A Show

I'm sitting here alone with a drink in my hand
Watching my favorite rock and roll band

I love it fast and I love it loud
It's like I'm the only one in the crowd

It's been one hell of a night and one hell of a show
When the clock strikes 12, I'm on a hell of a roll

It's been one hell of a time and one hell of a show
When my songs come on, I got to get up and go

I found my stage in a dark filled room
Plenty of shadows from this side of the moon

The lights turn up and the lights turn down
I'm dancing like a snake to the pungi sounds

It's been one hell of a night and one hell of a show
When the clock strikes 12, I'm on a hell of a roll

It's been one hell of a time and one hell of a show
When the sun comes up, I got to get up and go

One Hundred Days Of Rain

The clouds conceal the evidence
The sky is blackened thick
The birds no longer fly around
The sun is pale and sick

The heavens secrete unfiltered mist
The winds blow from the west
The moon inflames the other side
The hounds can sense the threat

Hurricanes and chronic pain
One hundred days of rain
Angry mobs and irate gods
Reign down on the terrain

The missing glare is silent
The planes vanish in thin air
The puff of smoke drifts away
The wide blue yonder disappears

The children count the lucky stars
The engine purrs like a train
The cattle gather under the tree
The shelter from the strain

Hurricanes and chronic pain
One hundred days of rain
Angry mobs and irate gods
Reign down on the terrain

One Snail Of A Life

When I'm all alone and scared of my own shadow
I crawl inside my shell to stay hidden from the world

I'm not always sluggish and I'm not always boring
I'm just a little slow in the wee hours of the morning

I always leave a trail so I can find my way home
On the back patio or thru the garden of gnomes

I'm not dangerous or contagious
Hell, I don't even bite
I'm just being slick
Living one snail of a life

Please have patience and just give me an inch
And I'll stick with you like a fresh bag of cement

I may be a little selfish, and yea I left pee on the pot
But you knew that when you married this smooth gastropod

You stay up late when I'm out eating bugs and roots
Cuz I always bring home flowers, algae and fruits

I'm not dangerous or contagious
Hell, I don't even bite
I'm just being slick
Living one snail of a life

One

I felt the cold wind blowing
Like Winter in my mind
I felt the shivers running
Up and down my spine

I drank the blood of children
I ate the spoiled food
I took your free handouts
Stole the sun and moon

I am a lonely number
I am the chosen one
I flirt with Mother Nature
Just like the devil's son

No ones where I'm from
I'm just one and done
Nothings adding up
Live and die as one

I saw the naked shadows
Like an evil vision
I saw the consequences
Of each wrong decision

I drink from dirty glasses
I eat from kitchen floors
I slip into your thoughts
Sliding in your back door

I am the perfect figure
I am the only one
I tease the fenced in dogs
Just like a pointed gun

No ones where I'm from
I'm just one and done
Nothings adding up
Live and die as one

I smell the hint of a death
Like a deadfall trap
I smell the fear of doom
The head and neck will snap

I bought my one-way ticket
I paid my way to the top
I pushed my own religion
Stirred the thicken plot

No ones where I'm from
I'm just one and done
Nothings adding up
Live and die as one

Paracosm

The children were playing in the rain using their imagination
To make believe the ground was lava and the puddles were salvation

They were rescued by a ship of sailors, storming thru the ocean seas
Bringing warm clothes, hot chocolate, cookies and herbal teas

My survival mechanism is to endure and live on
Living in a castle like a childhood paracosm

The sound of distant sirens calls them home for a night of sleep
Time to close the book of dreams, hope and creativity

The morning light delivers a brand-new world to explore
Where superheroes save the planet from a zombie war

My survival mechanism is to handle and hold on
Living like Peter Pan in a childhood paracosm

Poster Child

Another dose of happiness
That fell into my lap
I drink it down like Fanta
Then I take an hour nap

A tall glass of water
In a Cookware boiling pot
She points in the direction
Then I find her favorite spot

Sunshine, clear skies
Spicy hot and mild

Smooth skin, blue eyes
She's the perfect poster child

She likes to grab my arms
And handle me like lotion
So, we rub off on each other
And enjoy the local motion

Legs that stretch forever
A sexy V shaped back
She could be on billboards
Or a Glamour photograph

Sunshine, clear skies
Spicy hot and mild

Smooth skin, blue eyes
She's the perfect poster child

Pretty as a wildflower
Blowing in the breeze
Lovely as baby squirrel
Playing in the trees

Sun rise, long thighs
Running free and wild

Smooth skin, blue eyes
She's the perfect poster child

Pretty Little Lady

Innocent as a baby bird opening her eyes
Treacherous as a firecracker burning up the sky

Pretty little lady
Growing up so fast
A freckle with wings
Flying in first class

Pretty little lady
Marching down the street
When I look down from heaven
I'll never miss a beat

Sweeter than the frosting on a chocolate cake
Tougher than a mongoose pouncing on a snake

Pretty little lady
Hold onto my grip
I promise you forever
To never let you slip

Pretty little lady
Marching down the street
When I look down from heaven
I'll never miss a beat

Promised

Sparkling green eyes and big red lips
Golden charm and a southern accent

She comes from a place of holy divine
Where flowers grow tall in the fresh sunshine

I promised a love song written just for her
She can be Hemingway and I'll be the author

I promised to make her happy forever
And treat her like a cherished treasure

She traveled many miles on a bridge too far
Danced into the pages of my printed art

I followed her back to her bar stool seat
Then she smiled and knocked me off my feet

I promised her a future designed just for her
She can be the architect and I'll be the builder

I promised to sing her songs every night
Take her by the hand and make her feel alright

Psychedelic Motor Heads

Turn the music up and the lights down low
Hug a tree and blow some smoke

Harmony and good vibrations
Anytime, place or situation

Flower power and the Grateful Dead
Hippies, junkies and psychedelic motor heads

Touch of grey and keep on trucking
Casey Jones, fire on the mountain

Melody and dancing bears
Tie dye shirts and dreaded hair

Keep your face on straight
Don't flip your wigs
Be more like
Psychedelic motor heads

Make love not war and peaceful signs
Lightning skulls, turtles and fresh designs

Heaven, serene and unity
Come together like solidarity

Flower power and the Grateful Dead
Hippies, junkies and psychedelic motor heads

Reborn

In a world I did not create but will go on living as if it was my own making
I paint the night and draw the day and spend my lifetime pretending

Skip, jump and hop just to run away
Sing, act and dance just so I can play

Kick, scream and fight just to lock up horns
Read, rhyme and write just to feel reborn

I am not one to mince words, I sometimes speak in code
I always think twice but my tongue has a mind of its own

Talk, chat and jaw just so I can say
Drink, cuss and sin just so I can pray

Kick, scream and fight just to lock up horns
Read, rhyme and write just to feel reborn

Reinventing The Wheel

I'm reinventing the wheel
But I'm not your normal automobile
Faster than a speed demon
I ain't never been beaten

If you want to catch my eye
You better learn how to ride
If you want to travel in style
Better do your homework child

I'm better off without the friction
I had enough time to heal
I'm just remodeling myself
And reinventing the wheel

I'm reinventing the wheel
But I'm not your normal automobile
And when the sun hits me right
I'm shiny as a Christmas light

I got my plastic Jesus
He won't ever mislead us
I left the devil far behind
Because all he did was whine

I'm better off without the friction
I had enough time to heal
I'm just remodeling myself
And reinventing the wheel

River Of Life

With an Ace up my sleeve and two tens in my hand
I keep playing the cards the best way that I can

Rolling the dice
Splashing the pot
I hit the river of life
Against all odds

She kissed me good night and blew me some luck
Rubbed on my juju so my cards won't suck

Drinks on the house
And girls gone wild
I hit the river of life
With Hollywood style

I promised her earrings and dinner for two
She said win baby win and I love you

Out kicked my coverage
She's a walking cliche
I hit the river of life
And struck gold on the way

Romeo

You, her and me and that makes three
You know my name, I'm a VIP
I'm a long way from home, I'm a country star
I get head on the road cuz I play guitar
Learned how to love when I turned sixteen
I'm a Romeo and a bit obscene

I got an old RV and a parking spot
I get high all the time like an astronaut
My wife left me for another man
She caught me fucking in a mini van
I'm a motorboat fucking love machine
I'm a Romeo and a bit obscene

You can always find me at a topless club
Or making new friends at the local pub
I drink my dinner and I snort cocaine
Smoked more weed than Lebron James

I'm a lover not a fighter if you know what I mean
I'm a Romeo and a bit obscene

I shave my balls three days a week
Scrub my asshole squeaky clean
I fuck all night and watch porn all day
I like girl on girl but I'm not gay
I eat it fresh and sweet like a tangerine
I'm a Romeo and a bit obscene

Roulette

With a chip on my shoulder and a mouse in my pocket
We're flying thru life like a Space X rocket

I live for the moment, and I seize the day
I'm not here to work, I'm only here to play

Right here
Right now
I'm going to place my bet

Some how
Some way
I'm like a game of roulette

Living my life as if I was a real cartoon
I keep getting off track like a spinning typhoon

I live for today and not tomorrow
I count the numbers like Tony Soprano

Right here
Right now
I'm going to place my bet

Some how
Some way
I'm like a game of roulette

Bridge -
Black or red
Even or odd
But if you go green
You better win it all

Rub My Eyes

Hotter than a coffee pot
Sweeter than a lollipop
Cleaner than a whistle
Smelling like a flower shop

Smarter than an ornery fox
Cuter than a bunny hop
Fresher than a sea breeze
Breathtaking like a mountain top

Pretty as a sunrise
In the red, orange and pink sky
Lovely as a snowfall
Makes me want to rub my eyes

Funnier than a girl gone wild
Warmer than a child's smile
Brighter than a summer day
Wearing sunglasses with style

Sexier than a glamour shot
Stronger than a sailor's knot
Simpler than a schoolgirl
Playing in her favorite spot

Pretty as a sunrise
In the red, orange and pink sky
Lovely as a snowfall
Makes me want to rub my eyes

Rusty Bucket

I'm a hunk of junk, a snake and a skunk
An excuse of a person
And an unfortunate drunk

I'm a bad example and a rotten apple
A rat in the gutter
With an unfavorable struggle

You can fake it or suck it
Take it or leave it
I'm falling apart
I'm just a rusty bucket

You can see it and smell it
Like a big piece of bullshit
I'm wasting away
I'm just a rusty bucket

I'm squeaky, leaky and a little bitchy
Harsh and corrosive
And unflattering gritty

I'm worthless and clueless and a pile of rubbish
Taste like a lemon
With an unusual tarnish

You can fake it or suck it
Take it or leave it
I'm falling apart
I'm just a rusty bucket

You can see it and smell it
Like a big piece of bullshit
I'm wasting away
I'm just a rusty bucket

Sail To Be Free

Heading out to sea and I'm all alone
Got a case of beer and my fishing pole

Catching the wind that blows to the east
Riding the waves from the captain's seat

Some boats are built for size and speed
But I'm the guy that sails just to be free

Soaking up the sun in the middle of the day
Splashing my face while the dolphins play

Hooking a marlin is a sporting conflict
But throwing her back is the greatest gift

Some boats are built for size and speed
But I'm the guy that sails just to be free

Satan's Pet

I'm an odd-looking creature from the wilderness
I live in dark places and I'm indigenous

I'm on a diet full of anything
I eat crickets, roaches and chicken wings

Glowing eyes that stare you down
I'm camouflaged green and brown

I'm well known on the internet
I'm not cute but I'm Satan's pet

I'm more deadly than a cigarette
I can give you cancer, I'm Satan's pet

Eyebrow horns and wrinkly skin
I hang around on thorny twigs

I sometimes hide in your couch and chair
I've even scurried through your underwear

I skip to a beat and walk on water
I'm the loud badmouth behind your shoulder

I'm well known on the internet
I'm not cute but I'm Satan's pet

I'm more deadly than a cigarette
I can give you cancer, I'm Satan's pet

Shadow

I had him since he was just a little pup
His poor soul, was just to wound up

One day his little heart just gave out
Now I just want to cry and shout

I'll miss the shadow in the windowsill
I'll miss him running up and down the hill

You can't replace man's best friend
I never wanted it to ever end

Black as night but bright as day
A silly goose that loved to play

I'll miss the shadow in the woods
I'll miss him laying at my foot

Full of life and full of mischief
In the yard or in the kitchen

He brought us love and shared his toys
To all the stuffed animals that he destroyed

I'll miss the shadow behind my back
I'll miss his bark and loyal acts

Ship Of Fools

It was a disaster from the start, full of mischief and perversity
A ship run aground, stranded in stupidity

A wave of shattered dreams, crashing on the port side deck
Taken for a ride, on a ship about to wreck

Sailing high and sailing by
Sailing under the dark blue sky
Cruising on and cruising thru
I'm cruising on a ship of fools

No one more foolish than the rest, rash and simple minded
A crew lost at sea, broken and misguided

A mutiny and rebellion, on the sea of insurrection
The tail takes the lead, headed in the wrong direction

Sailing high and sailing by
Sailing under the dark blue sky
Cruising on and cruising thru
I'm cruising on a ship of fools

Shot Thru The Heart

Shoot the wings off a moving fly
Draw my weapon of choice
I make my own sort of luck
One of the good old boys

After a lifetime of bad habits
I'm trying to make a real difference
I got one more shot to take
You're on a need-to-know basis

Shot thru the heart again
I'm a killer of souls and men
Shot thru the heart again
Your mistake is my revenge

They made you just like me
And threw away the mold
A gangster with a heart
A copy and a clone

If you're in my line of sight
Then there's nowhere to escape
I bend bullets like a thug
Like a sniper taking aim

Shot thru the heart again
I'm a killer of souls and men
Shot thru the heart again
Your mistake is my revenge

Showtime

I wanted to go see a late-night show
So, I took a one way trip down to Mexico

Violence, murder, robbery
Sexual deeds and misogyny

The food was spicy and the beer was warm
As the show girls lined up to perform

Corrupt cops, drug trafficking
Rape, theft and kidnappings

Back alleyways and neon signs
I may be committing a serious crime
Time to show and time to tell
I may end up in a prison cell

My eyes wide open and my stomach weak
I couldn't believe the dancers' technique

Human smuggling, aggravated assault
Drug cartels and business fraud

The smoke was thicker than the LA smog
The night was hotter than a boiling frog

Enticing me with lots of twerking
Grinding hips and knee bone jerking

Back alleyways and neon signs
I may be committing a serious crime
Time to show and time to tell
I may end up in a prison cell

Sidewinder

You're a venomous trick and a two-time bitch
One hell of a ride and you scratched my itch

You slide over here and slide over there
When midnight comes you dare to bare

Yea here she comes
She's tons of fun
Yea there she goes
The legend grows

A sidewinder
A bump and grinder
Spit and bite
Like a desert viper

You're a lying brat and stretcher of facts
A prick in the arm and a pain in my ass

You slither here and you slither there
When nighttime comes, you're everywhere

Yea here she comes
She eats the crumbs
Yea there she goes
The black widow

A sidewinder
A bump and grinder
Slip and slide
Like a horny viper

Silent Storm

A face that smiles for no one
And eyes that pierce the soul
A mouth that preaches evil
And a large nose like a troll

Avoiding the sound of church bells
And the lightening in the sky
The demons try their best
To stay hidden out of sight

The silence moves in slowly
Like the cold inside the warm
The average death count rises
Like the trail of a silent storm

The silence rolls in slowly
Like the time it takes to mourn
The feeling (harm) goes on for miles
Like the trail of a silent storm

A tail stretched for generations
And claws that scrape the deck
A hideous head like a pig
And a prison tattoo on the neck

Hiding from the enemy
In the middle of the night
The monster turns to stone
If ever caught in sunlight

The silence moves in slowly
Like the cold inside the warm
The average death count rises
Like the trail of a silent storm

The silence rolls in slowly
Like the time it takes to mourn
The feeling (harm) goes on for miles
Like the trail of a silent storm

Sing Songs And Get Drunk

One-night things got a bit irate
Cuz, I came home just a little too late

She started acting all mean and rude
Like a rattler in one of those crazy moods

I guess I didn't show enough remorse
So, she packed up the spoons and the forks

I told her not to slam the dam door
Cuz I've seen this sideshow all before

Well, my guitar gently weeps
Cuz my women she done left me
And now my music- oh yea my music sets me free

Sometimes I don't have squat
No woman or a single pot
But that's ok, I don't need much
I sings songs and I get drunk

Three weeks later and I'm on the couch
I get a call from her running her mouth

She said this time she's gonna really hurt me
She took my credit card on a spending spree

I wasn't looking for a reason to fight
I can't help to think she took my dog for spite

She told me fuck off and go to hell
Now I'm alone and I don't know who to tell

Well, there's crying in the streets
Cuz I'm all alone in the sheets
And now my music- oh yea my music sets me free

Sometimes I don't have squat
No woman or an ounce of pot
But that's ok, I don't need much
I sings songs and I get drunk

Sinister Plot

Hide in plain sight
Wait for the bite
Just like a snake
Curl up and strike

A man on the stage
Educated with rage
Left his blood-marked
On history's page

Ready or not- The President's been shot
The signs and symptoms of a sinister plot

Ready or not- No one's been caught
The lightning bolt left a nation in shock

Stand by and watch
Lee Harvey Oswald
Hired by some
To win at all costs

They all act like crooks
Smooth with good looks
The bar has been set
And books have been cooked

Ready or not- The President's been shot
The signs and symptoms of a sinister plot

Ready or not- No one's been caught
The lightning bolt left a nation in shock

Bridge-
All of the rats and all of the snakes
Conspire together to hide the mistakes
They infest the swamps like disgusting roaches
Infiltrating the media, politics and showbiz

Start Me Up

I'm always looking for something more

Self-affliction or another score

You cast the line and I take the bait

If you're gonna bite me then I just can't wait

Start me up don't interrupt
Turn me on and pop the clutch

Start me up don't cut me off
I'll let you know when I had enough

You can take me home if you got the key

I got a feeling that it's just not me

You stick your needle into my skin

Like a drag of smoke that pulls me in

Start me up don't interrupt
Turn me on and pop the clutch

Start me up don't cut me off
I'll let you know when I had enough

Steering Wheel Guitar

The open road ahead is music to my ears Driving my salvation
until the boundaries disappear

Lord, you hear my thoughts screaming out my lungs
Filling up the pages with my faith, hope and love

I can feel your delicate death grip and your fingers running up
and down my arm
Turning me in ten million directions fretting me like a steering
wheel guitar

Stuck in traffic again
Rethinking my directions
Hands on my steering wheel guitar

Congested and blocked
Got to be a better way
Hands on my steering wheel guitar

Ride off in the sunset until the morning comes
Singing all night long until my voice is numb

Lord, you see the way to everywhere I've been
Playing me like a fiddle and a 5-string violin

I can feel your delicate death grip and your fingers running up
and down my arm
Turning me in ten million directions fretting me like a steering
wheel guitar

Stuck in traffic again
Rethinking my directions
Hands on my steering wheel guitar

Congested and blocked
Got to be a better way
Hands on my steering wheel guitar

Struck By Thunder

I heard you slip into the back of my house
Trying to be sneaky and quiet as a mouse

But you came in like a lion and left like a lamb
Higher than a cloud and blowing like a fan

It was a bang and a flash, a smash and a crash
More shocking than the voltage of a lightening blast

Struck by thunder, drenched by rain, spinning faster than a hurricane

I heard the crashing sounds of the kitchen plates
Like a 5-car collision on the interstate

My Pottery Barn vase never stood a chance
When she threw a fit like a long wooden lance

It was a bang and a flash, a smash and a crash
More shocking than the voltage of a lightening blast

Struck by thunder, drenched by rain, spinning faster than a hurricane

Sweet Temptations

Scream your final breath, drink your dying blood
Incapacitated, spiked, demoralized and drugged

Wake up to the blur of a thousand pounds of nails
Dropped off in the alleyway, three doors down from hell

Turn the lights down low and feel your sweet temptations
Empty out your pockets and fill your expectations

There ain't no magic pill to remember what you did
You keep playing round with fire in the playground that you live

The venom keeps you happy and coming back for more
It's like a new horizon that opens up the door

Turn the lights down low and feel your sweet temptations
Empty out your pockets and fill your expectations

Ten Minutes From Hollywood

Jump on the bus and head to LA
Passed-out bums get out of my way
The cracks on the street belong to me
I'm living out the Hollywood scene

John Wayne, Brad Pitt and James Dean
The Rock, Newman and George Clooney

They all been where I been and stood where I stood
I'm 10 minutes from Hollywood

Its dog eat dog all the way to the top
The bleeding hearts will never stop
I traded for blood and sold my soul
Played the part and broke the mold

Denzel, Cruise and DiCaprio
Marilyn, Bruce, and Al Pacino

They all been where I been and stood where I stood
I'm 10 minutes from Hollywood

I ate the scraps, and I slept around
Did what I did just to please the crowd
Swept up by the red-carpet dreams
All for fame and an ounce of gleam

Tom Hanks, Brando and Jolie
Feldman, Haim and Sean Connery

They all been where I been and stood where I stood
I'm 10 minutes from Hollywood

The Animal

I'm an instigator, exaggerator
King of the jungle and alligator

I chase down the weak
Relentless, mean and unsociable
They call me the animal
Desperate, wild and untamable

I'm an interrogator, suffocator
I get fumed easily like an exterminator

I cause lots of havoc
Bedlam, fights and turmoil
They call me the animal
Disturbed, lawless and big trouble

Bridge-
I chew with my mouth open
and lick my paws at the dinner table
Yea I was born in a barn but that don't make me unlovable

I'm a widow maker, terminator
Rip your heart in two breaker

The Best Smile In The Business

Let me take your picture and turn you into art
My hands can paint the flowers that stem inside your heart

Sight, magic and awesomeness
Oh child, you got the eyes of a hypnotist

Kindness, love and friendliness
Oh child, you got the best smile in the business

Let me taste your wine until I drink and drown
Your sweetness pours over me as I gulp it all down

Sight, magic and awesomeness
Oh child, you got the eyes of a hypnotist

Kindness, love and friendliness
Oh child, you got the best smile in the business

The Blackest Of All
Black Omens

Give the war to the dragons, burn the house of stone
Demolish and destroy it like a broken bone

Blood stains on the pillow your fingers left behind
The mark of the demon that fills your heart unkind

Bats, witches, black cats
Foreshadows of misfortune
An upside down cross
The blackest of all black omens

I traveled thru time; I've seen what hell is like
It's hotter than a lightning bolt and a match's strike

Dressed all in black, you're a shadow in society
Moving thru the kingdom, prowling ever quietly

Bats, witches, black cats
Foreshadows of misfortune
An upside down cross
The blackest of all black omens

Bridge-
There you sit alone
Like a raven on a throne

High above the castle
The devil and his gavel

The Devil's Mite

I met my match in a laundry mat
He was folding clothes next to where I sat

He looked around and lit one up
Started breathing fire like he owned the club

I saw his eyes and I starred him down
Broke his nose and threw him out

He bit my flesh, I felt the bite
I felt the power of the devil's mite

I traded sins for an instant win
Made peace with enemies only to lose my friends

I started over and never stopped
Fell down more times than a dam raindrop

I saw his teeth and I saw him frown
Sent him home with his crestfallen crown

His eyes were glass and black as night
I saw the power of the devil's mite

The Facebook Devil

He sneaks and he creeps, and he plants deceit
Acting all sweet like a normal freak

He acts like your friend
And he likes to meddle
I'm talking about
The FB devil

He shows up uninvited wearing a disguise
Slightly misguided and wiggles inside

He is self-proclaimed
And he thinks he's special
I'm talking about
The FB devil

You can't put him down he is always around
Selling his worship like a traveling clown

He likes to intrude
And he likes to bezzle
I'm talking about
The FB devil

You pay to be admired and look inspired
Displaying your voice like a church boy choir

He's an anarchist
And he's a running rebel
I'm talking about
The FB devil

The Gods

The gods can be cruel, mean and heartless
Fierce, bloodthirsty and merciless
They can strike without any warning with diabolical rage, and
nonsense

The gods can be vile, nasty and sadistic
Unsparingly spiteful and unsympathetic
They can be harsh and cold hearted with homicidal acts of
viciousness

The gods have their hero's and favorites
As they judge, rule and distract
The gods have already made up their minds
As they anticipate, and order an attack

The gods can be wicked, evil and demented
Childish, cold blooded and ruthless
They can ignore good and compassion with a demented portray
of savageness

The gods can be brutal, bitter and remorseless
Ugly, shocking and hideous
They can be painful and agonizing with inhumane methods of
dictatorship

The gods have their hero's and favorites
As they judge, rule and distract
The gods have already made up their minds
As they anticipate, and order an attack

The Master Plan

I chart the map and plot my next move
With romantic words and gentle grooves

I'm a historian of the artifacts
A masked crusader of wanton acts

Stand right up and walk right in
Lay down your arms and nod your head
Take my word and shake my hand
It's all a part of my master plan

Now I know just what to do
My formula is coming thru

My reputation is on the line
So, I do my best to make it shine

Stand right up and walk right in
Lay down your arms and nod your head

Take my word and shake my hand
It's all a part of my master plan

When I get tired of your perfume
I get a bad case of the switcharoo

I need more friends just like you
So, I can entertain your friendly crew

The Never Ending War

A story of battles but no resolution
A legal action but no prosecution

Heaven and hell
The endless war
Two armies fighting
To settle a score

All the campaigning is suffocating
It's growing bigger and it's escalating

All the bloodshed is forever bleeding
It keeps on churning and never ending

A body of problems but no solution
An ongoing match but no conclusion

Angels and demons
The heavenly host

Spiritual beings
Screaming like ghost

The dogs of war are marching and fighting
They bark all night, and they keep on biting

All the bloodshed is forever bleeding
It keeps on churning and never ending

The News Today

Comets, locust and solar eclipse
Tornadoes, earthquakes and viruses

Newspapers plagued with war and conflict
The evil dead rising from the crypt

I heard it on the news today
The end is near and underway
I saw it on the news today
The planet is in disarray

The blood rains down from the sky
Mountains sink and the water will rise

Men will come to force your hand
Sabotage and steal your land

I heard it on the news today
The end is near and underway
I saw it on the news today
The planet is in disarray

The Old Man and The Sea

Use me as chum
Throw me to bottom of the sea
The most beautiful way to go
Recycle and eat me

Take me out to sea or take me home
Either way brother I'm just skin and bones

I'm stuck in the current like a drowning flea
Like Moby Dick and the old man and the sea

I'm going to die on the most perfect day
Calmest seas we've ever seen
Send me to the gallows below
So, I can sink like a submarine

Washed up and left for dead
Crashing waves and rotten fish heads

I'm stuck in the current like a drowning flea
Like Moby Dick and the old man and the sea

St. Martin or The Grenadines
San Juan, Jamaica or in the Keys
Doesn't matter where I drown
Just tie me up and leave me be

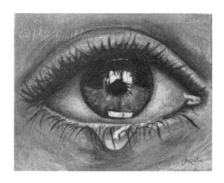

The Person It's Hard To Be

It's hard to shed a tear when you're on top of the hemisphere
One week and one day has passed me by

It's a blessing I'm still here when I could easily just disappear
Run away to sob my heart out and cry

So, if you find me laying down and sleeping on the job
Won't you please just wake me up and shield me from the boss

Be my savior I love and trust
Be my good fortune and my luck
I'll be person it's hard to be

Be the passion I seek and want
Be the energy and vibe I hunt
I'll be the person it's hard to be

It was almost quitting time when I decided to change my mind
I remembered which way I needed to go

It's good to be me sometimes when my spirit is feeling fine
Wave goodbye and find a friend to say hello

So, if you see me wondering around and lost all alone
Won't you please just take my hand and show me where to go

Be my savior I love and trust
Be my good fortune and my luck
I'll be person it's hard to be

Be the passion I seek and want
Be the energy and vibe I hunt
I'll be the person it's hard to be

The Rolling Stones
(broken dreams)

Wake up early and make my bed
Drinking gasoline just to get ahead

My broken dreams
Are bleeding me

Fill my pockets with cold hard cash
I'm flying high when I fly first class

My broken dreams
Are bleeding me

A handful of diamonds, dust and bones
Wild horses and The Rolling Stones

Money, drugs and all I've blown
Sister Morphine and The Rolling Stones

I'm venomous as a diamondback
I squeeze my victims when I attack

My broken dreams
Are killing me

The FBI knows me by my name
I'm the contaminate they like to blame

My broken dreams
Are killing me

A handful of diamonds, dust and bones
Wild horses and The Rolling Stones

Money, girls and all I've blown
Sister Morphine and The Rolling Stones

I lick my lips and I taste your taste
Smile, grin then I kiss your face

My broken dreams
Are bleeding me

I call you up when I'm all alone
Jumpin Jack Flash and The Rolling Stones

Dancing free in the pleasure dome
Brown Sugar and The Rolling Stones

The Spirit

The sounds in my head turned into words
So, I just wrote them down

I listened real good like a troubadour should
Running all around the town

I'm fire and ice
I'm feeling alright
The spirit rings in my brains

I'm bittersweet
Drinking gasoline
The spirit runs thru my veins

The fire burns deep in my wildest dreams
Woke me up in my bed

I sold my soul for some rock and roll
Played until my fingers bled

I'm fire and ice
I'm feeling alright
The spirit rings in my brains

I'm bittersweet
Drinking gasoline
The spirit runs thru my veins

The Wise Old Bull

The wise old bull was reliving his glory
When the strong young bull asked what is your story

Well, the wise old bull said I used to be in porn
Lived a good life and had a real longhorn

The strong young bull said you still look good for your age
You must have been a real stud back in the day

Well, the wise old bull thanked him for the nice kind words
Back in the day I used to get drunk and chase down the herd

The strong young bull laughed and nodded his head
I hope to accomplish at least half of what you did

The wise old bull said I have some advice for you to take
Live out your dreams before you become a cube steak

Well, the strong young bull stopped dead in his tracks
He said you may be right as a matter of fact

Then he said I will take your advice and pass it along
I know that you're wise and you would never steer me wrong

The wise old bull said son I think you may have what it takes
To turn hay into gold and find a good soul mate

I can see thru all your BS
Sniffing around the barn
I've known many equivocators
Spinning of the yarn

The Wizard

I came to see the wizard
And the magic of his ways
Got lost in the moment
Like a child in a maze

Just a man behind a curtain
With a secret to his name
Full of make-believe truths
Smoke, fire and some flames

Deliver me from evil
And take me to the wizard
I'm stuck in a nightmare
Like a pigeon in a blizzard

He dropped out of high school
And ran off to be a clown
Made a fortune playing tricks
In the villages and towns

He went over to the dark side
And fell off the spinning earth
Made friends with his shadow
Promised never to return

Deliver me from evil
And take me to the wizard
I'm stuck in a nightmare
Like a lizard in a blizzard

Thrill Of The Kill

Call me sunshine
Or lightening in a jar
I'm super-hot
And a burning star

Check out My Space
Or my Instagram
I'm a selfie queen
And a Facebook scam

I'm the life of the party and a socializer
A smoke alarm and a firecracker

I'm just here to bang and the thrill of the kill
When things get too hot, I run to the hills

Have a drink on me
Or a quiet dinner
Just light my fuse
And my skin gets hotter

Release the grip
Or pull the trigger
Hang around long
And feel the pressure

I'm a hard case to beat for any lawyer
A big red flag and a frequent flyer

I'm just here to bang and the thrill of the kill
When things get too serious, I run to the hills

Til I Die

I got a two-dollar bet on the edge of my seat
It cost me an arm and a leg

Goodfellas got me by the back of the neck
If I lose, I'm good as dead

Let it ride
Let it slide
Let it spin
Til I die

Watch me try
Watch me fly
Watch me win
Til I die

I got a special gift, but I don't like to brag
It's hard for me to lose

The wise guys hate to see me double down
Baby needs a new pair of shoes

Let it ride
Let it slide
Let it spin
Til I die

Watch me try
Watch me fly
Watch me win
Til I die

Time Of My Life

Drag me round and round
Chase you back and forth
Up and down the hallways
From the day you were born

You're the reason I get old
The logic when we fight
Even when I'm defeated
I'm having the time of my life

It hits me hard when you cry
Melts my heart when you laugh
The day that you outgrow me
Will tear my heart in half

Pretty, sweet and spoiled
You're my sugar and spice
Even when I'm frustrated
I'm having the time of my life

All the simple hooligans
I wouldn't trade it for the world
It gives me something to do
Just what the doctor ordered

Too Many Mouths To Feed

I'll be in town sometime next week
Hit me up down on the street

I told my friends all about your eyes
Mini skirt and black thigh highs

You got everything I want or need
But honey I got too many mouths to feed

I love how you dress up for the occasion
It tells me you got some coordination

I hope you're ready for an epic night
I know a place we can grab a bite

You got everything I want or need
But honey I got too many mouths to feed

Bridge-
You got nothing to fear
The line starts in the rear
Even if you're extravagant
As a crystal chandelier

Tricks Of The Trade

You can tell your best friend what she wants to hear
She can come along and be the souvenir

You're looking hot
Hot enough to blow up
You can strut around
Like a little show off

Come on pretty baby- you can pull my leg
You know all the ploys- and the tricks of the trade

I know you want to show me what I want to see
It will be the best time until you have to leave

You're looking sharp
Sharp enough to cut me
You can dance around
Footloose fancy free

Come on pretty baby- you can pull my leg
You know all the ploys- and the tricks of the trade

It's not enough to tease me every time you speak
I'll bring the flowers if you let me pinch those cheeks

You're looking sexy
Sexy in the shadows
You can prance around
When you wear the black hose

Come on pretty mama- no need to be afraid
You know all the games- and the tricks of the trade

Trust The King

When you reach the end there are no more first
You are the sum from everything you learnt

Been there, done that
Win, lose, cry, laugh

You can be proud of who you are and who you made
Trust the King, don't be afraid
You can follow him along the way
Trust the King, don't be afraid

When you pass the time by counting sheep
Hurry, wait until you fall asleep

Never empty, always full
Rich, mature and capable

You can be proud of who you are and who you made
Trust the King, don't be afraid
You can follow him along the way
Trust the King, don't be afraid

Hungry hearts, they call his name
Shout it loud, don't be ashamed

Forever young, growing old
Mother, father, I'm coming home

Underbelly

Across the world's deepest oceans
The winds and tides are set in motion

The serpent swims up from below
Alert the crew to face the foe

The kraken fetches fear and doom
Swings his arms like a sweeping broom

Fly by air or sail by sea
The path you're on is tough and deadly
Fly by air or sail by sea
But stay away from the underbelly

Around the world and around the globe
Life and death is the way it goes

The dragon's fire brings the devil's heat
His mouth is full with rows of teeth

The cyclone hovers with waves of rain
Sinking ships in a night of pain

Fly by air or sail by sea
The path you're on is tough and deadly
Fly by air or sail by sea
But stay away from the underbelly

Vengeful

Police trying to get me
Lock me up for good
Take me into custody
Treat me like a crook

I ain't got no friends
Jail mate kicked my ass
I ain't made for loving baby
I'm just full of crass

Now I'm vengeful
Tempered and out of mind
A little distasteful
Raving mad all the time

Diablo riding shotgun
Ares on the loose
Rile me up a bunch
I ain't got no excuse

I ain't much for talking
Can't carry a tune
I'll spend all night long baby
Howling at the moon

Now I'm vengeful
Tempered and out of mind
A little distasteful
Raving mad all the time

Head down on the pillow
Camera on the wall
I can't stop the rubbing baby
Man, I'm feeling raw

Now I'm vengeful
Petty and out of line
A little disdainful
Tit for tat all the time

Wanted Man

Anyplace I go
I'm part of the show
Ask the bartenders
They all know

There's nowhere to hide
I sit down inside
It's funny to me
When my worlds collide

I'm a wanted man
Oh yes, I am
I won't be denied
Until I'm buried alive

I plan for the best
Always ready for next
A price on my head
Get more for no less

Wheeling and dealing
Just one in a million
In a wink of an eye
I'm making a killin

I'm a wanted man
Oh yes, I am
I won't be denied
Until I'm buried alive

Welcome To Daytona

Eagle wings and daisies
Tattoos on display
Music from the eighties
Cool breeze comes my way

Spring break, hotels and sand
White butts, trash and beer cans

California to West Virginia
Tacoma to Pennsylvania
They do it all the same
But not like in Daytona

Big boobs and bikinis
Long, hot summer days
The bikers going crazy
They fight and disobey

Strip malls, beaches and suntans
Boardwalks, golf carts and race fans

Carolina to Arizona
Alabama to Oklahoma
They do it all the same
But not like in Daytona

Wet Dog

Woke up this morning naked and cold
Lost in the woods and all alone

A trail of blood with every step
Leading from the village to where I slept

The scraps in my teeth taste like steak
My stomach sickens like a bad headache

I'm like a wet dog, I scrounge, and I beg
I feel like biting someone's leg
I'm like a werewolf, I hunt for the thrill
The more I change the more I kill

The moon rises when the earth rotates
Revealing my body's inchoate state

When the night owl calls to me loud and clear
The wildlife scatters like frightened deer

When you see my shadow it's much too late
There's no retreat and no escape

I'm like a wet dog, I scrounge, and I beg
I feel like biting someone's leg
I'm like a werewolf, I hunt for the thrill
The more I change the more I kill

Whiskey Jim

He looks just like a pirate and smells just like one too
He murders men for hire and has a green anchor tattoo

Line it up
End to end
Drink it down
With Whiskey Jim

You can't out drink a drinker but you're welcome to join the crew
Partake in all the horseplay, chug and smoke all night thru

Rip you up
Limb from limb
Take one shot
To the chin

He never misses happy hour, in fact he hasn't moved in days
He just sits there like a bounty, sipping on his Grand Marnie

Line it up
End to end
Drink it down
With Whiskey Jim

You can pull up a seat and sit right next to him
Stay up past the witching hour and hang with Whiskey Jim

You Are My World

If I was a guitar made of rhythm and blues
I'd rock and roll you with my blue suede shoes

If I was a dragon with a fearsome attitude
I'd hunt, roar, growl and intimidate you

You are my friend you are my lover, and I will follow you forever
You are my world you are my power, that I'm waiting to discover

If I was a King with all the gold and the pearls
I'd slay all my enemies and buy you the world

If I was an Angel with wings and halo
I'd fly down from heaven and paint you Picasso

You are my friend you are my lover, and I will follow you forever
You are my world you are my power, that I'm waiting to discover

You Can't Be Good If
You're Never Bad

I know you want to
Squash me like a bug
Pull my wings off
Burn me in the sun

I know you want to
Send me to my room
Without my dinner
Beat me with a spoon

In between the good times
When you're feeling sad
You can't be good
Unless you do some bad

But don't you worry
And don't be sad
You can't be good
If you're never bad

I know you want to
Push me down the stairs
Eat my heart out
Like a lion or a bear

I know you want to
Run away from home
Smoke a cigarette
Act like you're all grown

In between the good times
When you're feeling sad
You can't be good
Unless you do some bad

But don't you worry
And don't be sad
You can't be good
If you're never bad

No one wants to be a thorn in the side
A crybaby or the reason to lie
It takes a little rain; it takes a little pain
to make the sunshine

You Keep My World Spinning

I'm flying high again
With the sky below my feet
Racing thru the clouds
So, we can finally meet

I'm leaving them behind
In a cloud of smoke and dust
The truth is in the cards
My face a royal flush

A match made in heaven
Blessed beyond the bounds
You keep my world spinning
Spinning round and round

You're a bird in the breeze
Singing many songs
Dancing in my dreams
Right where you belong

You're the sun and the shine
That heaven sent to me
It's written in the stars
For you and me to see

A match made in heaven
Blessed beyond the bounds
You keep my world spinning
Spinning round and round

Printed in the United States
by Baker & Taylor Publisher Services